Deceptive Performances

A Police Magician's ledger of Con Games

Glenn Hester
copyright Glenn Hester 2011

ISBN 978-1-257-64943-3

Foreword by:

Whit "Pop" Haydn
American Confidence Man

Dedications

To three brother officers who died while in service with the Glynn County Police Department in Brunswick/ Glynn County, Georgia

Lt. Ed "Cooter" Dixon
EOW   09/25/96

Officer Elmer Strickland
EOW   12/17/04

Capt. Jack Boyet
EOW   05/16/10

You were taken away from us way too soon.
Rest in Peace

Acknowledgements

Robert Steiner, Bruce Walstad, Whit (Pop) Haydn, Richard Bliss, David Hariton, Magic Ian Sutz, Dennis Marlock,, Professionals Against Confidence Crime, National Association of Bunco Investigators, and many others I have known throughout these years. Thank you for your contributions to this.

Special Mention to my Family

Bert and Joyce Hester RIP, Glenn B. Hester III RIP, Julie Hester, Janet Hester RIP, Beannie Foulke, Joyce Buckingham, Greg Hester, Kim Hester, Brianna Kichelle Hester RIP, Karen, Vince and Tyrus Jones, Christine, Kevin and Ciera Yarborough, Jaime, Kyler Tanner & Hillary Jones, Debbie Hester and Maria Chapman, who have lived with my con games for many years.

Special Thanks to:
Bob and Pam Hammer
PAM'S # 1 Law Enforcement Dinner Club
912-267-PAMS
4344 Highway 17 North
Brunswick, Georgia 31525
Thank you for being there for me and my family.
To reach PAM'S #1 on Facebook,
http://www.facebook.com/pages/Brunswick-GA/Pams-1/117012055013169?v=wall&ref=search

Foreword

I am a magician, and I lie and deceive for a living. But people pay to see me do it, and I would never take unfair advantage of anyone. However, I learn a lot from studying the psychology and methods of the con man and hustler that I can use to improve my own work.

I admire the con man for his cleverness, and for his skill, though not for his life choices. It is good for everyone to have a certain amount of knowledge about these things, just so that it improves your chances for not being a victim of these sorts of criminals. It happens much easier than you imagine.

You may have heard that it is "Impossible to cheat an honest man." This is true only in a few specific types of con games. Many con games take advantage of the trust and good will of people, or their lack of attention, just as effectively as those that depend on the victim being involved in an illegal scheme.

I have known Glenn Hester for several years. He is an expert at crooked carnival games and short cons, and has contributed greatly to my online Scoundrels Forum. This is a place where experts on gambling and con games, historians, writers and actors, along with magicians, card cheats, con men, three card monte and shell game players, carnival game cheats, and pool hustlers discuss all aspects of the soft rackets.

It isn't difficult to see how having a policeman in this strange brew could have been unsettling for some of the people involved. Yet Glenn made friends with everyone easily, and treated them all with respect, dignity and interest. He answered their questions and talked about how best to deal with police officers, and gave his own opinions on morality and the law. Glenn was always humane, kind and understanding no matter with whom he was dealing. I am proud to be his friend.

There are only two kinds of people in this world—suckers and people that can be had.

Everybody can be had, but the sucker will bet you fifty bucks he can't be had. Knowing you can be had, and knowing some of the ways that can happen, may keep you from becoming a victim.

This book tells you about some of the slickest schemes that you will ever hear about, some of them very entertaining in their cleverness.

Hopefully you will learn about them here…and avoid having to learn the same lesson the hard way.

--Pop Haydn

pop@pophaydn.com

Contents

Introduction

There are deceptive performances every day in our lives. Many will remember magic shows they attended. Deception in this art form is acceptable, but not in criminal activity. Con games have been around for many years.

You may have pulled a few cons in your day. As a child, I feigned sickness on days that I did not study and prepare for tests. As an adult, I pulled a few cons on my wife to save face in certain situations.

Deceptive performances are shown in many aspects of life. It can occur on the street, at your home, through media, or any other place where someone has contact with you. What I hope to achieve with this book is to share a few of the many confidence crimes that are played out around the states. Some are old classics while others are set to the times of our era.

As I have told many in lectures, with the con game you do not always know the intention of the con artist. If someone came up to you, pointed a gun or knife at you, and demanded your money, you would know their intentions. It is not so easy to see the intention of a con artist when you do not know they are getting ready to steal from you.

Con artists take you into their confidence and get you to play along until the con is realized. It is only afterward that you know you were taken in by a scam. Scams come in many forms and the scam artist plays the part so well, you are left feeling sick that you fell for such a flim flam. The sad part is, many do not report this to the local authorities. They are ashamed. When they don't report it, the crime goes unpunished and the offenders are left to take others down the road.

Some, who have reported these crimes, have lied about it to save face. I remember one such case with a person reporting they were robbed when the elements of a robbery did not exist. The victim was taken in by a Three Card Monte scam and lost all of the company's money.

We were able to locate the offenders and recover the money. It turned out they were a professional group from Ohio who has played this scam at many rest areas and truck stops along the Eastern Seaboard.

The victim was notified of the arrests and recovery of the money. Because the victim filed a false police report, saying that it was a robbery instead of telling us what really happened, the victim was arrested when returning to our area to recover the money.

As both a law enforcement officer and a magician, I

have studied deception in many forms. I remember, after instructing a class on con games to a group of officers, one officer made a remark that I could make more money if I switched sides.

I told him that I know I could, but I have a conscience. I cannot hurt someone and not have remorse about it. Many con artists do this day in and day out, without remorse, as this is a job to them. Just as we go to our daily work, they do the same.

It is sad that we have people in our lives who will hurt another, but that is a fact of life. It matters not how they are related to us, through friendship, blood or just people we meet, someone will do something to hurt you physically, emotionally or financially.

And it is financially and emotionally that we will show you in this book. The objective of the con artist is to take you for as much money as they can get. Some will do this in a short time, better known as a short con. Others will do this over a period of time, better known as the long con.

Sadly, some victim's are so devastated by the loss, they commit suicide. I have heard of some children putting their parents in nursing or assisted living centers, as they felt their parent could not take care of themselves because they were taken in by a professional con artist.

Personally, I feel they were upset with their parent because part of their inheritance was taken.

The victim's I have interviewed over the years have had some heartbreaking stories to tell. I have attempted to speak to family members to get them to understand that the con artist is good at what they do and not to blame the victim for falling for the scam.

I remember one such case where a lady lost a great deal of money to the Hanky Switch scam. She was so upset, that she almost did not report the crime. After listening to her, I helped her along with the report and told her that she was not at fault. Even though she thought she was going to make more money, she wound up losing her life savings, something she could not afford to do.

I spoke to her husband and explained what had happened. He was not a happy camper about this, as I would imagine. However, he did understand that these people were professionals and his wife, having no knowledge of scams, fell victim to them. Sadly, we did not locate the offenders or recover her money. All that we had from the scheme was a handkerchief and rolled up paper to resemble the money inside it.

What I stress to you is this; be cautious about going into something that sounds too good to be true. Human nature does not permit us to share "found money" with a stranger. And, if that stranger wants you to put up "good faith money", that should be a red flag that something is not right.

I have been asked if I have ever been conned. I will reveal it now. I remember working in a news and record shop as a young man. A client came in wanting to purchase a magazine. He paid with a large bill. During the transaction, he kept asking me to change the bills. This, unknown to me at the time, was a Change Raising scam.

After the confusion and tallying the register, I found that the offender took around forty dollars from me during that short time. I felt ashamed and mad that I was taken in by such a smooth talker. It was at that time that I did not believe the saying "the customer is always right".

And, yes, I have been conned later in life. I have been married and divorced three times. Seriously, any of us can be conned. When you think you are too smart to be conned, that is when it will hit you hard. Be alert; be aware, there are people out there looking for their prey. Don't be a victim, be smart. The only way to keep from being a victim is not to be involved with it in the first place.

Chapter 1

Understanding the Con Game

P. T. Barnum said it best when he was quoted as saying "Every man is a damn fool for five minutes a day; Wisdom comes from not exceeding the limit". We all make mistakes in life. Some we learn from, others we continue to make. When we have learned from these mistakes, we gain wisdom.

Another quote that tells us about con games comes from Damon Runyon from "The Idyll of Miss Sarah Brown". "Son, no matter how far you travel, or how smart you get, always remember this. Someday, somewhere, a man is going to come up to you and show you a brand new deck of cards, on which the seal is never broken. And this man is going to bet you that the Jack of Spades will jump out of the deck and squirt cider in your ear. But son, do not bet him, for as sure as you do, you will get an earful of cider."

This tells us that if a "deal is too good to be true, it probably is". Con games have been classified as a special kind of cheating. Magic principles have been employed to get the con across. I am not going to reveal any magic secrets, but to mention certain principles used.

Let us look at what a con game has been called. Bruce Walstad, in his seminars on confidence crime, has described the following:

1) A specialized kind of Cheating

2) A well rehearsed play

3) A method of making the victim give money to the con artist
4) Always controlled by the con artist, although the victim may feel they are in control

5) Sometimes played to convince the victim they are involved in criminal activity

What better way to make sure the victim does not report this to the police than to make them think they have committed a crime. Believe it or not, there have been people, who come from a low gene pool, who have reported crimes they were involved with. I remember one such person making a report about a threat he received from a drug dealer that he had bought drugs from.

Motivations that make a con game work are:

1) Large amounts of money shown

2) A victim is convinced that they cannot lose on this

3) The appearance and acting ability of the con artist

4) The victim trusts someone who is out to do them wrong

5) And in most cases, the victim's greed.

In the Introduction, I mentioned the short and long con. The short con is played out from just a few minutes to a few hours where the long con can extend out several days, weeks or months. The "Sweetheart Swindle" is one of those long cons whereas the "Pigeon Drop" is a short con.

There are two types of con artists. One such is those that know they are conning you. These people intentionally swindle you. The other is one who has conned themselves. This is the person who believes in something, be it a product or service, and wants you to be in on it as well. Some of these so called work at home businesses are part of this con.

Regardless if they know they are conning you or not, both of these con artists actions can have devastating results for the victim. Remember, the con artist is very convincing. Many are good at human psychology and can pick a victim out of a crowd.

It is human nature to want something for nothing. Think about this; if you are approached by a stranger, who tells you he or she found some money in an envelope and does not know what to do with it, what would you do? Most honest people would try to find out who the owner is.

In some cases, there may be a note showing the money is illegal, such as gambling money or drug money. This puts the idea in the mind of the victim that the money will not be reported as missing. Now, if you take the bait and play along, think about this; why would you need to put money of your own up if money is already shown?

In the classic Pigeon Drop and Hanky Switch scams, this is the premise for the con. Again, this should be a red flag, or as the FBI says, a clue, that something is not right. Does greed take over as you feel you will receive something for nothing? Yes. Is this a deal too good to be true? Yes. Does your ear feel wet from the Jack of Spades that squirted cider in it? Then you have been a victim of a con game otherwise known as a deceptive performance.

Let's keep our ears dry, our eyes open and our minds sharp. If you want a free ride in life, have someone pay for you to ride the ferris wheel at the next carnival you visit. It is the only free ride you will get.

Any deal or investment should be looked at carefully before going into it. Investigate whether the risk is good or bad. The same holds true when offered a chance to make hundreds or thousands of dollars in a con game. Take the time to think about what you are doing. When you do this, you will see whether you should go ahead or stop dead in your tracks. When you have time to think, you won't end up with the stink.

Chapter 2

Street Scams

As the title shows, these are scams that occur on the streets, or anywhere outside your home. They can be played in rest areas, on corners, in front of businesses or in back alleys.

PIGEON DROP

This is the oldest of all the scams that dates back over 400 years. where the con was known as "Ring Falling". In today's society, a victim will be approached by a stranger who will start up "casual" conversation or they may even just ask if the victim dropped a bag or envelope. Either way, the hook is introduced by showing the victim a large sum of money that was found.

Sometimes, a second con artist, otherwise known as a "shill" or "confederate" will come on scene and pretend they do not know the first con artist. All three have to agree to put up "good faith money" so each can trust the other. A note may be shown that the money is illegal such as stolen, gambling or drug money, which will not be reported as missing.

The money the victim gives them will be placed in the

bag or envelope and sealed. During this time, a principle of magic will be employed and the misdirection done will switch the bag or envelope for a duplicate one, which will be given to the victim to hold.

A location and time to meet and split the money will be given. The victim, who has hold of what he or she believes to be the money, will arrive at the designated venue at the time requested. After waiting for a good while, and no one shows up, the victim, curious about the contents of the package, will open it only to find paper in it.

The money the victim put up will be gone along with the con artists who scammed the victim.

THREE CARD MONTE

Some people feel this is a gambling scam. I assure you, it is not gambling. In gambling, there is a chance you can win. With this, there is no chance of your winning. The intention of this so called game is to steal your money. Anyone found winning this game can be considered a secret player or a "shill".

Three cards are shown, two the same and one different. Your objective is to pick the different card, such as a Queen. A magic principle of "sleight of hand" is used along with "misdirection" to achieve the objective of this game.

The card tosser will shuffle the three cards around on a makeshift table while giving some cute patter. You attempt to locate the card to win the game after putting down your money. After losing, you may be introduced to the person who shows he or she knows how the game is played.

Now you are being suckered in by a shill. They will tell you where the Queen is all the time while you do not play. When you do, you will lose. They may even use the ruse of the "bent corner of the card". This is where the Queen is bent, showing you where it is at all times.

Sadly, if you fall for that ruse, you will soon find out that the Queen's bent corner was straightened out and another cards corner was bent. Remember, these people are good at what they do, or they would not be in business.
On a personal note, when the Three Card Monte gang from Ohio was arrested, one of them did a demonstration for us at the station. The other officers picked the wrong card. Knowing how this was done, I picked the right card each time. I wanted the tosser to think I was lucky until one of the officers blurted out that I was a magician and knew this game.

HANKY SWITCH

Similar to the Pigeon Drop, this uses a handkerchief instead of a bag or envelope. You come in contact with someone who pretends they are not from America. Inside a handkerchief is shown a large amount of money. The victim is enticed to pray with the stranger who asks for their help as they do not trust banks.

Again, a second con artist, pretending they do not know the stranger, will arrive and offer to help. Like the Pigeon Drop, the victim will take money out of their account via ATM or at the bank and place it inside the handkerchief which will be secured, switched and given to the victim to hold. Again, the victim will realize they have been conned only after time has passed and they open the handkerchief to find paper inside.

SHELL AND PEA

Similar to the Three Card Monte, this uses a pea and either walnut shells or bottle caps which will hide the pea while being moved around. The victim places his or her money down and attempts to guess which shell or cap the pea is under.

To summarize, like Three Card Monte, you will not win at this game either. In most cases, the pea will not be under any of the caps or shells as it is secured in their hand. They will place it under a cap or shell only to show you that you guessed wrong. Again, sleight of hand and misdirection are magic principles used to get the con across.

CAR WASH

Some people, too busy to take time out of their day to get their vehicles cleaned, will attempt to find a person who will come to them and clean their car. Some of these businesses will clean the car at the person's home, business or take it to their location where it can be detailed.

Most are honest businesses that provide this service, but there are some who look for ways to take advantage of the situation. Think about this; did you leave keys to your home or business in the car? How about your checkbook or ATM card?

There have been cases reported of financial transaction fraud soon after having the vehicle cleaned. What about burglaries to your office or home? Duplicate keys made during that time allow the offender to steal from the places he or she knows you are not present at the time.

Then, there is the other scenario; your car has been stolen. You will only realize that when the detailer fails to return it to you at the designated time he or she told you they would. Some cars have been traded for drugs. Never leave any personal info or keys or access codes in your vehicle when having it cleaned. This is a crime of opportunity for those who want to make something off of it. This goes for taking it to legitimate car washes as well.

ROCKS IN A BOX

Also known as "The Block Hustle", the victim is led to believe that the sealed goods they are buying are actually inside the box. The victim is shown an actual VCR, DVD player, Camcorder or other item on display. The seller gives some excuse as to why the price is so low.

They may even mention it being stolen goods. When the victim takes the package home and opens it up, all that is shown inside the box are rocks or some other heavy object that makes the box feel like it had the real item inside.

JEWELRY SALES

Want to buy gold jewelry at a bargain price? Con artists on the street know this, so they do their best to sell it to you. Gold chains or other items are for sale at a cheap price on the streets. Some may even promote them as being stolen through a snatch and rob if they are broken.

Your best bet is to forget about looking for a bargin on the streets when it comes to gold or other jewelry. And if you do succumb to making a purchase, have it appraised. You will find that the so called gold necklace is nothing more than a copy of the real thing and worth nothing.

COIN SCAM

A stranger will come up to you and show you an envelope with what appears to be old and rare coins. They will use any number of ruses such as not being able to read and having you call a phone number for them that is listed on a piece of paper.

Unknown to you is the person on the other end of the call is also in on the con. The person you called will tell you that there is a reward for the return of those coins and give you an address to bring them to him or her.

The victim will be told how much the reward is. Now comes the part if the victim will be honest or crooked. Do you take the other person with you to collect the reward or do you offer him or her some of the reward? If the former, the finder of the coins will give excuses why they cannot go to collect and ask if you can split the reward with them. You go to the bank or ATM and take out the money agreed upon and give it to the finder of the coins. If the latter, which it will be in most cases, the victim may try to screw the finder of the coins and give them a little of the money from their own pocket or through an ATM transaction.

The victim will take possession of the coins and go to the address given only to find no such person is there. Depending on how much the reward for the coins was stated, and how much the victim gave the finder of the coins will determine how much money they lost to this scam.

LOST DIAMOND RING

This scam is similar to the coin scam. There are two different ways this scam is played. One way of doing this is for the victim to buy the ring when they find out there is a reward for its return. Like the coin scam, whatever money is given to the finder is gone when the victim finds out no such person exists at the address given.

The second way of playing this is to plant a ring inside a store. The con artist, who planted it, will find it and ask the clerk about it. Not knowing whose ring it is, the clerk will not know what to do. A few minutes later, the clerk will get a call from a frantic person stating they lost their valuable ring inside their store.

The clerk will state that someone did find it and attempt to locate the finder of the ring, who is still inside the store. The clerk will tell the caller that a person does have it and wants to know what to do. The caller will tell the clerk to use money from the business to give the finder of the ring and for the clerk to take possession of it.

Then, after work, the clerk is to bring the ring to a certain address and turn it over to the caller for a bigger reward. Needless to say, some clerks have been fired or even prosecuted for stealing money from a business doing this. Like shooting fish in a barrel, right?

LOTTO SCAM

With so many states having a lottery, and the jackpot being so high, this scam flourishes. Some con artists will come up to the victim stating they have a winning lottery ticket, be it a scratch off or online ticket. They will ask if the victim would like to buy the ticket as they cannot cash it in due to being wanted by the police or an illegal alien from another country.

The ticket will hold the winning numbers, but not for that day or it can be a forged scratch off ticket that was made on a computer since technology has advanced so much in these past few years. And, if you try to cash it in, you may be the subject of an investigation for having an altered ticket.

NIGHT DEPOSIT SCAM

In some cases, you will see an "Out of Order" sign placed over the night drop and a metal box in its place that has a sign telling you to make the deposit there.

I hope you are not that gullible, but some were. Also be alert to some ATM machines that may be altered to read your transactions to include your PIN or credit card numbers. With the advancement of technology today, con artists use this info as well.

ATM SCAM

As mentioned, this can happen as well. A piece of electronic equipment will be placed over the card skimmer to record info you put in it. A camera may do the "shoulder surfing" people use to do in the past, to record your transactions and info.

MOVING DAY SCAM

This is one of the cruelest cons I have heard about. Imagine thinking you will move into a home or apartment only to find it has been rented to several other people as well. Now that you have relocated and have no other place to go, what do you do?

How this works is the con artist will get the first month's rent plus a security deposit from several prospects. Then, each will be given a day they can move in. When several people show up at the same time, confusion is dominant, fights may break out among the renters and no one will know who has the right to move in. Sadly, when the real owners are contacted, it will be found that no one has gotten permission to rent the place.

Chapter 3

Home Scams

As the title states, these are scams that occur in or with your home.

BANK EXAMINER SCAM

The victim will get a call from someone claiming to be law enforcement or a bank examiner and asks them to assist in an investigation of a suspected teller. As most people are glad to help, many will agree.

The victim will be instructed to go to the bank and use a certain window designated and withdraw a certain amount of money from their account. Afterward, the victim will be met at their house by a person or persons who they spoke with on the phone. These people will take the money under the premise of returning it to the victim after the investigation is complete.

Just remember, no law enforcement or banking officials will ever ask you to use your own money in an investigation. This scam began back in the early 1960's. In this scam, the victim is not shown to have greed as there is no compensation for the assistance of the victim. Their reward, they think, is doing their civic duty.

BADGE PLAY COMEBACK

As with most names sold when you buy a product, con artists sell your name to other con artists so they can hit you again. If you have been the victim of a Bank Examiner or Pigeon Drop scam, you may be called upon again by so called law enforcement officials.
Con artists, posing as law enforcement, will contact the victim and let them know they were a victim of either of the above mentioned scams. They will tell the victim they have the criminals in custody and need their help to close the case on them.

The victim is led through this role again and withdraws money to assist the law enforcement officials. Again, the victim is burned as the money withdrawn is gone.
Again, no compensation for the victim, only doing their civic duty is their reward. This is a cruel con on someone who already has lost a good deal of money once before.

FOUND PET

Many people love their pets and when one goes missing, they put an alert in newspaper or online about it. As such, some con artists read about it and devised a scheme to take money from the victim. Sadly, no pet is found or returned.

The victim will get a call from someone claiming to have found their pet, but they are in another state. The victim is told that the caller needs them to send them money so they can ship the pet back to them. Western Union or another form of wire transfer is requested. Where the money is sent may not be the location of the con artist as money can be wired anywhere using a certain code.

After some time when the victim does not receive the pet, they will realize that they have been taken in by a scam. They are out whatever money they sent and may not trust a real call coming in if the pet is found.

HOME INVASIONS

Normally, a group of organized criminals, such as Travelers or Gypsies are known to do this type scam. However, others have been involved with it as well. That is why it is important for locals to call the police when they see suspicious activity in their neighborhood. If you see a vehicle driving around slow in the area, try to obtain a description of the vehicle and tag, if possible, to relay to the local officials so they can stop and identity the individuals inside.

How this scam works is the con artist will approach the victim under any number of ruses such as doing home repair, an IRS Agent, someone from the Social Security office, etc. Once inside, the victim is distracted for awhile while others ransack through the house and steal whatever valuables they can get in that short time.

It is always wise to never allow anyone inside your home, especially if you are female and live alone. Other crimes could occur to you such as assault or rape.

HOME REPAIR

Many, on a fixed income, cannot afford the current prices to fix up their home. Con artists know this and use any number of ruses to get you to hire them to do whatever repairs are needed.

One of the classic scams is the driveway sealant. The victim is shown the cracks in the driveway and told that the seller can use some of the sealant they have left over to repair the cracks and give the driveway a new look. The price is agreed upon and work begins. The work is shoddy, the sealant never dries and the victim is out whatever money expended for the work.

Roof repair is a classic as well as the victim is unable to go up on the roof to inspect whatever work was done. There are many other scams involving home repair. Just remember that a deal too good to be true is just that; too good to be true. Use only those people who are known to you, not a stranger. Again, anyone coming to your home is an invitation to disaster to your home or you.

COD SCAM

Con artists will deliver a package to your home while you are away. They will need a signature and money, so where do they go? To a neighbor's home who most likely will sign for the package, pay for it and deliver it to you to get reimbursed, as that is what good neighbors do, right?

This so called favor will cause you and your neighbor to be at odds when they find out you were not expecting any package and you are not going to pay them. Some, on the other hand, have accepted the package from the neighbor, paid them and found out nothing was inside. This causes hard feelings among neighbors as well.

It is best to notify any neighbor if you are expecting a package coming in that may need a signature. If it is COD, then money can be given to pay for the package ahead of time if you won't be home. Never accept anything from anyone where you have to sign for it or pay for it without permission of that person first.

OBITUARY HUSTLE

One of the cruelest cons on someone who just lost a loved one is having a package delivered to the home, in the deceased person's name. Thinking that the loved one ordered something before they died, the victim will pay for it only to find something that has no value or rocks in it for weight.

Another scam relating to this is a bill for services rendered and the con artist attempting to collect on it. This can range from auto repair to a number of ruses used that would show money is owed prior to the deceased persons passing.

WIRE FRAUD

The victim gets a call in the middle of the night claiming a relative, who is out of town, is in trouble or needs help. The ruse is a problem with law enforcement, car trouble, or any other ruse that would seem acceptable.

The victim needs to wire money, via Western Union, to an address out of state to help the relative. This scam has been prevalent in our area several times. Confirm the facts before sending any money.

PHONE, MAIL, INTERNET FRAUD

Have you gotten calls, mail or emails stating you were a winner of some contest you did not enter? Many have, and some have been gullible enough to send money to pay the taxes, etc. so they can claim their prize.

Have you gotten emails saying someone died and wants to ask your assistance with the money left? This scam still goes on today, and the sad part is, some fall for it. It is good to have a big heart and want to help, but dealing with someone unknown to you is a clue that something is amiss.

Never offer to help if they contacted you. Some will use religious speaking to get at those who feel they are doing God's Will. Remember the Stranger Danger programs mentioned to you when you were a child, the same cautions hold true as an adult.

Chapter 4

RETAIL SCAMS

Although some products are not up to par, we will deal with the criminal element with this topic.

YOU'RE FIRED

I don't see how this can happen, but it has. This is a bold scam played out on well known retail stores who have chains in many areas. The con artist will come into the store claiming to work security for that company.

Using any number of ruses, bogus problems with the store will be mentioned and the management will be ordered to hand over the keys to the store to the con artist. If the manager believes the con artist and hands the keys over, they are told they are fired and to leave.

Once the manager leaves, stealing goods and money is all that is left for the con artists. Again, I don't see how this works, but I understand it has happened. Should this ever occur to you, check the facts first before handing over the keys.

STORE DIVERSIONS

This has occurred in our area several times in the past. This scam is done mostly by Gypsy men and women with children. The Gypsies will cause a distraction in the store and get the employee's, especially the manager, away from the front office or other area where the safe is kept.

While the manager and employees are taking care of the situation, others will steal from the safe. Don't overlook the children as they have had the money stuffed in their pants or diapers. As quickly as the diversion began, it will end when the theft is completed. Never leave an open safe unguarded.

NEED CHANGE SCAM

Someone, claiming to work at a neighboring store, will come in and ask if they can exchange rolls of quarters for paper money. Several hundred dollars of rolled coins is shown and exchanged for paper money.

When opened, all that will be found will be quarters adorning the outside of the rolls and washers filling the inside of the rolls. It is best to refuse them and have them go to their bank to exchange it. Don't worry about hurting their feelings, as they do not work at any of the stores close to you.

BAIT & SWITCH SCAM

A product will be advertised with a good price for a special time only. When you go to the store, you will be shown a similar product that is not up to the quality of the one advertised.

The excuse will be they sold out quickly of that one and will offer to sell you another one, similar to the advertised one, at a lower price. Contact your Consumers Affair agency if this occurs.

SHORT/CHANGE RAISING

Short changing is when the customer gets back less money than what is really owed. In this case, the cashier would be the offender.

Change raising is when the customer gets back more money than is owed. The customer is the offender on this. Both rely on confusion and misdirection to work. Doing only one transaction at a time will help stop this theft.

Some say this is the perfect crime as either offender can always claim they made a mistake. Proving intent on either's part is always hard to do.

I mentioned, in the introduction, how I got clipped for forty dollars when I worked at a news and record shop many years ago. I know firsthand how this occurs and how I felt afterward. It is a horrible feeling.

TAKE IT OR LEAVE IT

The offender will hold back a part of the change owed the customer. If nothing is said and the customer walks away, the offender makes a profit. Even if a little change is kept, over a period of time it adds up.

If the customer says something, again, the offender can feign a mistake, apologize and all is forgiven. This can occur anywhere where someone gives you change from a purchase.

Some use the Bill Fold scam with this as well. The offender will count out the customers change, using paper money, but will use one or two bills that are counted out twice since they are folded. Always count your change to make sure you got the correct amount back.

Another aspect of this is the Hold Out. Coins are transferred from one hand of the offender to the other and given to the victim. In the process, a magic principle of "palming" is used to hold on to a coin or two. Again, this adds up over a period of time.

Although you witnessed your change being counted, remember to count it once you get it to make sure it is accurate.

TILL TAPPING

I was fortunate to assist in a video on this for the National Association of Bunco Investigators many years ago. This is a bold scam that shows how "palming" is used to steal large bills from a cash register.

The con artist will give the ploy that they do not understand the denomination of bills when making a purchase. They actually put their hands in the register and extract the larger denominations of bills.

They will hold it in front of the face of the cashier, asking questions about the denominations of the bills. While they do that, they will fold and palm a bill or two as they give back the rest of the bills to the cashier. Quite an interesting scam to witness. Never allow anyone to put their hands in your cash register. Remember, the customer is not always right!!!

Chapter 5

Paranormal Phenomenon Scams

FRAUDULENT FAITH HEALERS

I use the term, fraudulent, when describing the faith healers in this section because some know they are conning you. On a personal note, I do believe God does heal some people, but not all. I personally would not go to a healer as I feel the relationship between a person and God is personal.

A faith healer is someone who claims to cure a person of an illness or disease through the intercession with God. Each healer has their own style of performance and delivery in this ritual. If you watch these televangelists on television, you will see each of them doing this ritual.

Even if they are sincere, they may be wrong as they do not speak for God. Our Supreme Court decided that when a lady sued one such healer when her husband died of cancer. The faith healer promised, in God's name, that if the lady would send him money for his ministry, her husband would be cured.

The man did die; she sued and won her case against this so called faith healer. And the sad part is, he is still on television doing the same thing he did throughout the years, asking for money. Funny how each Bible verse he spouts has to do with "sowing the seed".

Seeing how these people "heal" others is likened to seeing a stage magician performing an illusion. Many, who are really sick, are told to leave their medicines alone and rely on God's healing. That is well and good, except some need the medicine to sustain life.
Those that got worse are told that they have a lack of faith, which is an out used by many when they cannot prove they helped heal the person through God. Some use the "calling out" method where they use common names and illnesses which could apply to most anyone.

Others have even gotten high tech using an ear device where someone backstage would read off the prayer cards a person's name, illness and address. If you ever watched Steve Martin in "Leap of Faith" that segment was shown due to the expose' of one such healer. In James Randi's book, "The Faith Healers", he and a team of other magicians are shown exposing this one healer using the ear piece, along with other exposures of other so called healers.

PSYCHIC SURGERY

Using a magician's principle of sleight of hand, these so called healers pretend to extract the disease tissue from the person and heal them of the illness or disease. This began in the Philippines, but has been practiced in the United States, illegally, as well.

If you ever watched the movie with Jim Carrey as Andy Kaufman, near the end of the show, you will see Carrey, as Kaufman, going to such a healer for this surgery. The method of the scam is shown, much too late for the star.

On a personal note, I have been used for this demonstration as well. While attending a conference for the Professionals Against Confidence Crime in Chicago many years ago, I was "randomly" chosen to assist Bob Steiner. Bob is the author of "Don't Get Taken" and Past National President of the Society of American Magicians. Bob also assisted James Randi in the exposure of the healer with the ear piece and has done many shows exposing others as well.

Bob went through the ritual of extracting certain objects from my stomach, after applying a red in color dye on my belly, which was supposed to be a cleanser. After I got up and went to the bathroom to clean up, Bob, who was already in the rest room washing his hands, was asked by me if he knew how wet he got my pants and underwear when he drowned me with the liquid?

Bob told me to put paper towels in my pants and that

should help. A person, from another convention, came out of one of the stalls. You should have seen his face when he witnessed Bob, who had red all over his hands and red all over my stomach area. As this person walked by our convention, he asked what PACC stood for.

I told him it stood for "Proctologists Association of Central Chicago". Bob and I still get a laugh for that nowadays. Bob also pretends to be a psychic at times for television shows, which will be described in the next section.

PSYCHICS

This contains two types of con artists as well. One who really believes they have such a power and the other who knows they do not have this power, but will con you out of your money as well.

A person who claims to be a psychic will tell a client things about them that may or may not help them. Some of what they say will be things that the client will want to hear. Places this power does not work is in the stock market, the race track, the lottery and other places where you gamble.

Some people are so into this that they will follow each direction given them by the psychic and not make a move without their advice. These people have no control over their lives as they rely on the psychic to guide them. Even on television, with the disclaimer, "FOR ENTERTAINMENT PURPOSES ONLY", people still fall for this.

Psychics claim to be in touch with the spiritual world or other world's to be able to have this power. I have witnessed such crap when I went to a psychic fair in a neighboring state. Using my stone face and not dressing in any attire that would reveal anything about me, I sat for a reading and did not confirm or deny any of the statements the so called psychic was telling me.

Needless to say, the psychic was getting frustrated with me as he needed affirmation to continue to hit on something about me. I would not give him that opportunity. To make a long story short, the psychic finally told me he was having trouble reading me (DUH) as there was a blockage or force not allowing him to get through (yeah, it was my stone face and no emotion shown on anything he said).

You may have seen certain people on television who claim to be able to talk to the deceased. I consider this a cruel con as there is no verification that they actually did speak with a departed loved one. There are a couple of well known people who do this. Whether they really believe they can or they know they are conning us, I don't know. Regardless, it is sad that they think they can give comfort to others with this so called power.

Don't forget the pet psychics. They claim to be able to communicate with your animals to find out things about them so you can take better care of your pet. Some, nowadays, call themselves "Animal Communicators" instead of pet psychics.
Just think about this first before running off to consult a psychic. Does it make any sense that someone else can speak to the dead or tell you how to live your life? Do you want them to control your every action? Take charge of your own life and make your own decisions. There is nothing wrong with you wanting to speak with deceased loved ones, but I doubt they will communicate back.

People have even used psychics in police matters, such as locating a person or body. The psychics would say that the body is located near water. Where on Earth does not have some water by it? If found near a lake or stream, they claim a hit. If found in a basement with pipes that have water in it, they claim a hit. Using psychics for police matters is a waste of time and manpower as the statements will not be relevant and cause precious time lost that could have been used to save or locate the victim.

FORTUNE TELLERS

Many are Gypsy women who have set up shop to do Tarot Card readings, palm readings, spiritual readings or whatever they choose to specialize in.

Most, nowadays, go under the guise of being called a psychic instead of fortune teller as it sounds more modern and not as spooky or dirty. They will tell you about your past, present and future. They have been called "the poor man's psychiatrist".

Some use a technique known as "Cold Reading" to make a person believe in their power. This is nothing more than a good acting ability and being alert to the person's response after each statement via body language as well as their verbal affirmations. Generalized statements are given and those that cause a reaction are hit upon again for the affirmation.

If you listen to them, you will really see that they are not "telling" you anything about yourself, but "asking" you. People with problems on health, sexual or financial matters are the most prone to being victims of this scam.

If you ever read the life of Harry Houdini, you would see how he exposed many of those, known as Mediums, back in his day, because he knew how they were tricking the public. Fortune tellers have used the skull in the egg trick, changing the color of water and other methods to continue with their client.

These tricks employ principles of science and magic. They also show the fortune teller how gullible a person is so they can continue to clean them out of their money. For entertainment purposes only, this can be a fun experience. To really believe and continue with this can be a devastating experience.

As mentioned earlier, Bob Steiner has gone on television shows claiming to be a psychic. He would amaze the audience with his powers only to reveal later that it was a trick. Some audience members got upset being duped, but they learned a great lesson, and no one was out of their money for it, unlike those using people who really claim this power.

Chapter 6

CRIMES AGAINST THE ELDERLY

Thankfully, many states have laws on the books to help protect our elderly. Sadly, some came way too late. The elderly have been targets for con artists for many, many years. Here are some reasons why they are chosen:

- Large amounts of money are sometimes kept in their homes

- Most are always home and accessible to the con artist

- Many are lonely and eager to talk with someone

- Many, due to their upbringing, trust strangers who show them some interest

- With a limited income, any good deal sounds inviting

- Age sometimes diminishes perception

- Some lack the knowledge of certain things

- Some will not be able to identify the offenders

- Some will not report the crime

Although this is not a complete list, here are some of the most common scams that apply to the elderly:

- Home Repair
- Sweetheart Swindle (showing love, then stealing all their money)

- Medical Fraud (products and services for the elderly)

- Faith Healing

- Fortune Telling

- Phone or Mail fraud (Internet as well if they use a computer)

- Consumer Fraud

- Bank Examiner Scam

- Badge Play Comeback Scam

- Psychic Surgery

As mentioned earlier, some are afraid to report the crime as they fear their children will think they cannot take care of themselves and place them in an assisted living or nursing home.

Others may just give up on life and commit suicide as they have lost all their savings and cannot earn more money with a job. For anyone who has had a parent fall victim to con artists, remember this; anyone can become a victim of a scam, even you. Now, would you want to be placed in an institution if that happened to you?

Chapter 7

GYPSIES AND TRAVELERS

Sadly, most people get these two groups confused because many of the crimes are similar in nature and some look almost alike, but there is a difference. Each has their own style of stealing.

GYPSIES

This group migrated from India around 1000 A.D. into Asia and then into Europe. They arrived in the United States sometime during the 1600's after being deported from England, Ireland, France and Spain. It is said that the first documented case of a Gypsy arrest in North America occurred in 1695 in Virginia.

If you have ever used the word "Gyp" or have been told you were "Gypped" out of something, this word comes from the word "Gypsy". It means to be swindled by them. Gypsies appear as natives of India as they have dark or olive complexions.

Sometimes, they are mistaken for people of Greek or Hispanic origin. Males are the dominant heads of the households and females are considered a lower class. Those, not of this origin, are looked down upon with little or no regard.

When I was in Chicago for a convention, Bruce Walstad introduced me to one such Gypsy. In fact, we all met at a restaurant and had dinner. I was amazed at how this "King of the Gypsies" had no problems telling me about some of the scams he and "his boys" pulled on people.

I found out that he could not read or write, paid cash for everything and lived in a mansion. Since he knew I was a cop, he asked for my business card, which I gave him. Bruce told me that was a mistake, which I found out later after returning home to Georgia.

This Gypsy telephoned me at the department wanting to know if I knew any cops in another jurisdiction. I told him I did. He went on to explain that some of "his boys" got arrested for doing home invasions in that area and wanted me to talk with the investigator to see if a deal could be worked out instead of them going to trial.

He told me that he was willing to pay back any money the victim's lost, plus a little extra for their time and trouble. When I spoke with the investigator about this, I was informed that the District Attorney was intent on prosecuting them as the D. A.'s mother was one of the victim's. Needless to say, the King was not too happy to hear that.

There are five basic groups of Gypsies in America.

Listed below are the groups and some of the scams they do:

1) American;

   * Home Repair
   * Ruse Entry (Home Invasion)
   * Fortune Telling
   * Shoplifting
   * Check and Credit Card Fraud
   * Insurance Scams (staged accidents, etc.)
   * Burglaries
   * Carnival Fraud

2) Yugoslavian;
   * Store Diversions
   * Shoplifting
   * Till Tapping

3) Polish;

   * Burglaries
   * Home Invasions
   * Shoplifting
   * Till Tapping

4) Canadian;

   * Tool Coating

* Insurance Fraud

5) Spanish;

   * Fortune Telling
   * Shoplifting

It is said that the American Gypsies are the largest group of people in the United States. It is also said that they hardly ever pay taxes, partake in US Census or even vote. As a result of this, they are known as "The Invisible Americans".

TRAVELERS

The group I am familiar with is those who live in Murphy's Village, South Carolina, just over the bridge from my hometown of Augusta, Georgia. Their village is named for a Catholic priest who said Mass for them, Fr. Murphy.

I went to a Catholic high school with some of them in the late 60's and early 70's. I also had dealings with them before their village had mansions erected and it was just a few mobile homes scattered about. They are an interesting bunch to deal with on a law enforcement level.

While I was employed in Brunswick/Glynn County,

Georgia with the county police, one of my cousins came down from Augusta to take possession of a truck that the Travelers financed through his company. We had just arrested several of the Travelers for scamming people with the driveway sealant scam. One victim was the mother of one of our officers.

The 3 basic groups of Travelers that reside in the United States are as follows, along with the scams they commit:

1) Irish;

* Home Repair
* Tool and Shop equipment sales
* Ruse Entry (home invasions)
* R.V. travel sales
* Sale of rugs, lace, purses, floor coverings, etc.
* Shoplifting

2) Scottish;

* Home Repair
* Ruse Entry
* R.V. travel sales
* Shoplifting

3) English;

* Home Repair

* Shoplifting

This is by no means a complete list, but does show some of the more popular scams they commit. Both Gypsies and Travelers are known as "Organized Crime" by law enforcement around the states.

Chapter 8

OTHER SCAMS

There are many other scams out there being played on unsuspecting victims. They can happen to anyone at anytime and anywhere.

Some of the other scams could be considered through medical fraud, carnival fraud, products sold on the television, otherwise known as infomercials.

There are laws to protect you and law enforcement agencies for local, state and federal jurisdictions that can assist if these happen to you.

I don't have a complete list of all the scams being played out in our nation, but this is a short synopsis of some of the more popular ones that have occurred.

Always research anything you are getting into, be it an investment, a product, a service or anything else where you may not have the knowledge needed to make an informed decision. Always ask those in the know about something you have no knowledge on.

Chapter 9

PREVENTION TIPS

First and foremost, before you jump into any so called great deal, think about it first. When you have time to think and research it, it will be shown for what it really is. Be alert for one or more of the following:

1) Anyone who tells you that they have found money and will share it with you, provided you put up "good faith" money

2) Anyone who wants to see the money for a short time and will return it to you

3) Anyone who offers you something for nothing

4) Anyone calling you on the phone, claiming to be an official, and starts to question you about your bank and other personal information

5) Anyone pushing you to make a withdrawal from your checking or savings account

6) Anyone who has a deal so good that you need to act fast or risk losing out

7) Anyone who tells you to keep a deal a secret

8) Anyone who asks you questions about your habits such as where you shop, what items you choose, etc.

9) Anyone who says they can get rid of your problems by performing a ritual that will involve a fee

10) Anyone coming to your door and claiming to be a utility worker, law enforcement or some other job description and wants entry into your home

11) Anyone who has merchandise for sale at a great price for a limited time only

The above list, although not complete, are red flags for you to stop and think about before going into it. Remember, taking time to think about what you are about to do will save you a lot of heartache and money.

RESOURCES:

BOOKS & WEBSITES

The following are a list of books for you to purchase and study if you want to know more about the different types of fraud committed. I highly recommend each of these books. I suggest you go onto the internet to look up where you can purchase them.

Should you not be able to locate the source for purchase, email me at policemagician@yahoo.com and I will email you where you can obtain it.

Books

Games You Can't Lose   Harry Anderson and Turk Pipkin

Gypsy Talk - Law Enforcement Guide to the Secret Language of the American Gypsy   Dennis Marlock

License to Steal - Traveling Con Artists: Their Games, Their Rules, Your Money   Dennis Marlock & John Dowling

The Change Raisers   W.M Tucker

Scams, Swindles and Rip Offs   Graham Mott

How to become a Professional Con Artist   Dennis Marlock

Don't Get Taken!   Robert Steiner

Scam! Inside America's Con Artist Clan   Don Wright

Sting Shift   Lindsey Smith and Bruce Walstad

Keeping Carnies Honest   Lindsey Smith and Bruce Walstad

Flim Flam   James Randi

The Faith Healers   James Randi

Robbery on the Midway   Tom Rinaldo

The Secrets of Amusement Park Games Revealed Brian Richardson

All About Carnivals   Gene Sorrows

Carnival Games: The Perfect Crimes   Richard Margittay

Carnival Secrets   Matthew Gryczan

Carnival Games: $10,000, 000,000 Hoodwink Racket Richard Margittay

The Con: How Scams Work, Why you're Vulnerable and How to Protect Yourself   James Munton & Jelita McLeod.

Carnival Cop   Glenn Hester

Websites

http://www.nabihq.org/en-us/index.php?sf_jst=r
National Association of Bunco Investigators (speakers on bunco)

http://www.policemagic.com/
Police Magic (info on lectures and books)

http://www.scoundrelsforum.com/
Scoundrels Forum (good info on scams and other con games by real con artists, magicians and others)

http://www.fraudtech.bizland.com/

Good info on all types of con games

http://www.magicsam.com/
Society of American Magicians (also has Paranormal Investigation Committee for paranormal investigations)

For Consumer Affairs, check with your state's Attorney General's office

About the Author

Glenn Hester started his law enforcement career in 1983 when he joined the Sullivan County Sheriff's Office in Monticello, New York. He moved back to his native state of Georgia in 1988 and joined the Glynn County Police Department in Brunswick, Georgia.

Glenn has been involved in magic since he was a young lad, but got serious with it after meeting a Franciscan Priest who showed him sleight of hand tricks. During his law enforcement career, he researched all types of con games and found that many used principles of magic to deceive victims. He took reports and investigated several claims of fraud, which came in different forms of scams. Glenn lectured and instructed many civilian and law enforcement personnel on the many types of scams being played in the United States. Glenn has been conned, himself, having been married and divorced three times, and having children and grandchildren who would fleece him and his wallet over the years. The biggest theft they committed was stealing his heart.

In Memory of

Retired Lt. Ed "Booger"

Barber

July 6, 2011

www.ingramcontent.com/pod-product-compliance
Lightning Source LLC
Chambersburg PA
CBHW021254280526
45784CB00005B/2368